O9-BHI-405

MONSTERS in MYTH

THE CHIMAERA

Monsters in MYTH

Titles in the Series

MONSTERS in MYTH

THE CHIMAERA

AMELIA LAROCHE

PUBLISHERS

P.O. BOX 196
HOCKESSIN, DELAWARE 19707
VISIT US ON THE WEB: WWW.MITCHELLLANE.COM
COMMENTS? EMAIL US: MITCHELLLANE@MITCHELLLANE.COM

Mitchell Lane

PUBLISHERS

Printing   1   2   3   4   5   6   7   8   9

Library of Congress Cataloging-in-Publication Data
LaRoche, Amelia.
  The Chimaera / By Amelia LaRoche.
      p. cm. —(Monsters in myth)
  Includes bibliographical references and index.
  ISBN 978-1-58415-925-4 (library bound)
  1. Chimera (Greek mythology)—Juvenile literature. I. Title.
  BL820.C57L37 2011
  398.20938'0469—dc22

                                                                    2010011151

ABOUT THE AUTHOR: Amelia LaRoche has been fascinated by the goings-on of the ancient world ever since she read the book *Greek Slave Boy* by Lillian Carroll at the age of ten. She finds the Chimaera intriguing, and as someone who often sees both sides of a story, she was compelled to put slightly less monstrous faces on this three-headed creature. This is her third book for Mitchell Lane Publishers. She lives in New England with parrots and a dog.

AUTHOR'S NOTE: The author's retelling of the Chimaera myth is based on other versions, but the dialogue and specific events are imagined—just as much of the dialogue and events in myths is imagined.

PUBLISHER'S NOTE: This story is based on the author's extensive research, which she believes to be accurate. Documentation of such research is contained on page 46.
    The internet sites referenced herein were active as of the publication date. Due to the fleeting nature of some web sites, we cannot guarantee they will all be active when you are reading this book.
    To reflect current usage, we have chosen to use the secular era designations BCE ("before the common era") and CE ("of the common era") instead of the traditional designations BC ("before Christ") and AD (*anno Domini,* "in the year of the Lord").

PLB

TABLE OF CONTENTS

MONSTERS IN MYTH

CHIMAERA

The Chimaera's father was Typhon (Typhaon, Typhoeus, Typhus), and his father was Tartarus. In this Etruscan mural from the Tomb of Oreus, Typhon's legs are serpents. He is bracing himself beneath the land, and his constant struggle causes Mount Etna to roar.

CHIMAERA

CHAPTER 1

A Beautiful Baby

Echidna (eh-KID-nah) held up a small piece of highly polished brass and admired her reflection. Her lively eyes sparkled. Her cheeks were smooth as marble. The half-nymph ran her fingers through her long hair, and wet her lips.

"I never get a day older," she murmured with delight.

She wanted to look lovely for Typhon (TY-fon) when he arrived. Normally Echidna used just her beautiful face and graceful upper body to lure travelers into her cave. She kept her lower half hidden, because that part of her body was a thick, speckled snake. Once the travelers were in her lair, she ate them raw and sucked on their bones.

Typhon got different treatment. For him, she had only soft kisses and tender words. And now she had good news for the fearsome giant.

Minutes later the earth shook as her monstrous mate slithered and stomped up to the cave, his dirty hair blowing in the wind. Even after he tucked in his huge wings, he could barely squeeze inside. Dragon heads sprang from his arms, and his eyes flashed brighter than lightning. Like Echidna's, his lower body was inhuman. Two muscular snakes uncoiled from his thighs.

Typhon roared like a hungry lion when he saw his beautiful partner, and a lick of fire curled out of his mouth.

"Be careful!" Echidna scolded. "You mustn't scorch my pretty skin."

The giant hung his head in shame and the snakes that were his legs let out sad hisses.

"Don't fret, my love. I forgive you," Echidna said. She patted his hairy cheek. "I have something wonderful to tell you. We're going to have another child."

Typhon grinned happily, then quickly wiped away the blob of lava that dribbled onto his chin before Echidna could scold him again.

Soon after, Echidna gave birth to the Chimaera (ky-MAYR-uh). She was born with a lion's head and body. From the middle of her spine rose a she-goat's head. Goat udders dangled from her belly. Her tail was a writhing snake. She could breathe fire out of all three of her mouths, a trait she inherited from her father.

Like most mothers, Echidna thought her new baby was beautiful.

The Chimaera's Parents

The Chimaera's name is spelled many ways, including *Chimera* and *Khimaira*. Her name means "she-goat."

Her father, Typhon or Typhoeus, was the son of Gaia (the Greek version of "Mother Earth") and Tartarus (a god, and also the name of a gloomy prison enclosed in bronze found in the underworld, where evil-doers—including gods and monsters—were punished).

Typhon is described in an ancient encyclopedia of Greek myths called the *Bibliotheca,* or *The Library,* as "a hybrid between man and beast. In size and strength he surpassed all the offspring of Earth . . . and his head often brushed the stars."[1]

He was so strong he could tear up mountains and hurl them at the gods and goddesses who resided on Mount Olympus. The king of the gods, Zeus, fought back. When Typhon ripped Mount Etna from the ground and threw it, Zeus hit it with thunderbolts. The mountain tumbled onto Typhon, where he was pinned for eternity, breathing lava and smoke through its top.

The Chimaera's mother was Echidna, which means "she-viper." The Greeks called her the mother of all monsters. Echidna hid in a cave with her offspring during Typhon's battle with Zeus. The victorious god let them live because he knew they'd come in handy as a challenge to future heroes.

Depending on which version of the story is read, Echidna's parents were the same as her mate's, which means Typhon was her brother. In other versions, he is her uncle.

Echidna never aged, but she was not immortal. She was killed in her sleep by Argus Panoptes (pan-OP-teez; "all-seeing"), a giant with one hundred eyes. In some myths, she was condemned to Tartarus in the afterlife.

Who Needs Monsters?

Fearsome monsters have been brought to life since people first started writing stories. The Japanese spoke of the terrifying Oni, flying demons with long fingernails and horns on their foreheads. They hunted for the souls of people who had committed evil acts. The Norse feared Fenrir (FEN-reer), a gigantic and ferocious monster in the shape of a wolf that scared the gods so badly they chained him to a rock deep under the earth. The Chinese had the Sin-you, with its sheep's body and shaggy mane. It could tell at a glance if someone was lying, and it would use the sharp horn in the middle of its forehead to pierce the liar's heart.

An 1865 engraving by Gustave Doré, called *Destruction of Leviathan*, shows the beast being struck down by God.

The Old Testament of the Bible mentions the Leviathan (leh-VY-uh-thin), an enormous, coiled sea monster that is described like this in the Book of Job: "Out of his mouth go burning lamps, and sparks of fire leap out. Out of his nostrils goeth smoke, as out of a seething pot or caldron."[2]

Perhaps some of the best-known mythological creatures come from the ancient Greeks, who filled their stories with monsters that were a mix of animal and human parts. One animal whose parts often appear in Greek mythology is the serpent, or snake.

"Each time the serpent was seen . . . it shot horrible fear through the hearts of those that challenged the monster as well as those the monster ravaged," write Katherine McCartney and Dr. Michael Delahoyde of Washington State University. "Throughout the centuries, the serpent has generally symbolized some sort of evil, whether monstrous, as in Greek and Roman mythology, or as the symbol of the devil, as in Christianity."[3]

Another common animal body part the Greeks used for their monsters came from the lion. The Sphinx, for example, was a reclining lion with a woman's head. This monster guarded the gates of Thebes and, until she was foiled by Oedipus (EH-dih-pus), strangled and then ate travelers who could not answer her riddle. A sister of the Chimaera, the Greek Sphinx also had wings and a serpent for a tail. (The idea of the sphinx originated in ancient Egypt; its lore was carried to Greece, Persia, and Asia.)

McCartney and Delahoyde say monsters with lion parts might represent man's inner savage: "This could possibly depict savagery and a hunger for blood from the hunt. These beings were considered monstrous because not only did they have

This sphinx, dating from 530 BCE, once marked the grave of two young people in a historical region of Greece called Attica, which contained Athens, the current capital. It now resides at the Metropolitan Museum of Art in New York City.

animalistic appendages, they also were brutally savage and loved the kill."[4]

The lion part could also stand for "a fear of pagans, cannibals, and uncivilized people—even the uncivilized urges within us,"[5] they write.

McCartney and Delahoyde ask an important question: "But why animals?" They suggest that people were afraid of their own nature, "because it makes them uncivilized. The beings with mixed animal and human appendages were savage and uncivilized. The monsters depicted pure animalistic nature, which civilized human beings received with disgust and revulsion."[6]

Many scholars say the monsters of Greek myth were put there simply so that people could kill them and become heroes. One of the greatest Greek heroes, Heracles (HAYR-uh-kleez), known to the Romans as Hercules (HER-kyoo-leez), was given the task of killing some of the monstrous offspring of Typhon and Echidna.

"Of course the mythical monster is present in any number of shapes . . . but they are there only to give the hero his meed of glory. What could a hero do in a world without them?"[7] asks Edith Hamilton in the introduction to her book *Mythology*.

Hamilton points out that in earlier mythology, the gods and goddesses were inhuman and even bestial. Some stalked the earth with animal heads or bodies. Others were towering beings whose thoughts could never be known by people.

The Greeks, however, made their gods and goddesses human and that "naturally made heaven a pleasantly familiar place,"[8] where people felt at home, Hamilton says.

Not only did the Greek gods and goddesses take human form, they were the supermodels of their day. One only has to look at statues made during the classical period to see that they were people's idea of perfect human beauty.

Myths starring gorgeous gods and goddesses became even more exciting when they included monsters that were not wholly human. Having features like hair made out of snakes or the creepy ability to breathe fire or drool poison made them different, dangerous, and scary.

Turning gods and goddesses into familiar figures and making the monsters easy to spot is one thing that set the Greeks apart from earlier mythmakers. According to Hamilton, "That is the miracle of Greek mythology—a humanized world, men freed from the paralyzing fear of an omnipotent Unknown. The terrifying incomprehensibilities which were worshipped elsewhere, and the fearsome spirits with which earth, air and sea swarmed, were banned from Greece."[9]

Heracles, whose life Hamilton calls "one long combat against preposterous monsters,"[10] lived in Thebes, an actual city in Greece. He was a hometown hero who seemed real to the people who heard about his brave feats.

Hamilton calls Heracles a symbol of Greece itself. "He fought the monsters and freed the earth from them just as Greece freed the earth from the monstrous idea of the inhuman supreme over the human."[11]

Was the Chimaera born to give a "hero his meed of glory"? If so, who would be the one to vanquish her?

Hercules is pitted against Achelous, a Greek river god, in this 1824 statue by French sculptor François Joseph Bosio. It can be seen at the Louvre, a museum in Paris.

The Chimaera's Siblings

The Hydra

Together, Echidna and Typhon gave birth to many monsters, including the Sphinx, the Nemean (NEE-mee-an) Lion, the Lernean Hydra (LER-nee-an HY-druh), and Cerberus (SER-ber-us). (Some myths say the Nemean Lion was born from Typhon alone.)

Driven mad by the jealous goddess, Hera, the hero Hercules murdered his wife and children. As punishment, he was given twelve labors to perform. One labor was to kill the Nemean Lion and bring back its fur. The lion's hide was impossible to pierce with arrows, so Heracles strangled the beast in his strong arms, and then skinned it with its own claws. He wore the hide as armor.

His second labor was to kill the Lernean Hydra, a serpent who lived in a murky swamp near Lerna. She had nine heads that dripped and spit venom. With the help of his nephew, Heracles cut off the heads and burned the Hydra's necks with a torch so that new heads couldn't spring up. He cut the Hydra's dead body open and dipped his arrows in her poison for later use.

Cerberus was a three-headed watchdog that guarded the entrance to Hades (HAY-deez), the land of the dead. In some depictions his tail is a snake, like that of his sister. Cerberus allowed spirits to enter Hades, but he didn't let them out. One exception was Orpheus, who charmed Cerberus by playing a lyre. Another was Heracles, who got permission from Hades, the ruler of the Underworld, to bring Cerberus to the surface. Heracles dragged Cerberus to the king who had assigned him his twelve labors. The king was so scared of Cerberus that he promised to release Heracles from his labors—on the condition that he drag the monster back to Hades.

This plate showing the Chimaera was probably made between 350 and 340 BCE in a Greek settlement in Apulia, a region in southeastern Italy where such pottery was common. It is housed at the Louvre.

CHIMAERA

CHAPTER 2

Time to Feast

The Chimaera slowly woke up and blinked her cold, yellow eyes. She stood and stretched her lion's legs. Her sharp, deadly claws scraped the cave floor.

She'd had the most delicious dream. In it, she had bounded into a small village and gobbled up two tender children, three cows, and an old peddler. The peddler had been full of gristle, and she'd had to work her jaws furiously to chew him to bits. Then she'd gleefully ignited every hut in the village with her fiery breath.

She stretched again, and her stomach growled. Today she would act out her dream, she decided. She hadn't eaten in days. It was getting harder and harder to find food. She'd raided most of the countryside around her cave in the mountain.

She padded over to a small pool of water at the side of the cave and lapped up a mouthful of cool, clear liquid. The goat's head rising from the middle of her back yawned and let out a small burp of fire. Her snake tail writhed around, flicking its forked tongue and peering at the scorched walls of the cave.

Stupid goat and stupider snake, she thought. All they did was complain. The goat was always bleating hungrily, begging for its belly to be filled. The snake had a foul temper, hissing and snapping at her hind legs when she didn't eat enough.

They weren't any company for the Chimaera. No one could be. There was no one else like her in the world. Sometimes she felt proud of that. More often, lately, she felt sad. She realized with a sudden pang that hit her somewhere between her lion's heart and goat's belly that she was lonely.

She lifted her head from the pool, and water dripped off her whiskers. As the last drops made rings in the pool, she caught sight of her reflection.

Her body was bigger than any male lion's. Her mane was thick and wavy—unlike any female's. Her brown goat's head sported sharp, curling horns. Her hind legs were covered in blackish green scales, and her writhing serpent tail ended in a dangerous slit-eyed head with sharp fangs.

"Eeeeeat," the goat bleated.

"Sssssssoooon!" the snake hissed.

"Shut up, both of you," the Chimaera roared.

Flames shot from her mouth and blackened another large patch of cave wall. She took a last drink of water to soothe her parched throat. Breathing fire made her thirsty.

She strolled to the opening of her cave and stared out at the breaking day. Thick forests covered the land below her. To the left and right, jagged peaks rose around her mountain. In the distance, the blue sea twinkled under the rising sun.

Today will be a good day, she decided. *A good day indeed.* No more lolling around the cave, feeling sorry for herself, wishing her grumbling stomach was filled. Today she would feast.

What Are Myths and Why Do We Have Them?

A myth is a story that explains how and why things came to be. This includes things we can see, such as the earth, humans, animals, and the stars. It also includes things we can't see, such as customs and religious beliefs. The Greeks believed these stories were true.

Even before humans could write down their stories, they passed them on verbally. Skilled storytellers wove exciting tales that made sense out of things people couldn't understand. Why do crops grow? What makes the sun rise in the morning and set at night? What happens to us after we die? Why are we here in the first place?

When people ask questions like these, they feel strong emotions. Myths are a way of controlling them with rational thought. By explaining the unknown, myths make life easier to understand. Think about how when you were small, you would lie in bed and see a scary shadow. It seemed like an unknown monster coming to steal you into the night. When your mother or father walked into the room and switched on the light, you could see that the shadow was made by something real, like a shirt slung over a chair. Suddenly, the shadow wasn't as scary—because you understood it.

Myths gave meaning to people's lives as well. The gods and goddesses directed life, death, and the afterlife. People felt comforted by believing that beings who were big, strong, and all-knowing were running things, and that the world was as it should be.

Myths also told people how to behave. For example, the story of Narcissus (nar-SIH-sus) tells of a boy so handsome, he couldn't stop staring at his own reflection in a pool of water where he was taking a drink. He eventually died because he wouldn't quit gazing at himself long enough to eat. Where he lay, a flower grew; it is called the narcissus. This myth warned people about vanity. People adopted his name to describe those who think too highly of themselves. They are called narcissists (NAR-sih-sists).

For many Greeks, myths did more than explain the unknown and give purpose to their lives. The stories were entertaining. Hearing a talented speaker spin a tale about a hero fighting a monster or of a god falling in love was equivalent to going to an action movie or a romantic comedy today.

Myths are not just ancient stories. In the

In Italian artist Caravaggio's 1599 painting, Narcissus gazes at his reflection, falling in love with it. In some versions of the myth, once he realized the reflection was his own and that he couldn't act on his love, he beat his own body until he died.

In a more modern myth, George Washington killed his father's favorite tree, but he told the truth about what he did and was forgiven.

1800s, Parson Mason Locke Weems told a tale about George Washington that illustrated the importance of being honest. When George was six years old, he was given a shiny new hatchet. George chopped the bark off his father's favorite cherry tree, and the tree died. When his father asked who had killed the tree, George cried, "I cannot tell a lie, father, you know I cannot tell a lie! I did cut it with my little hatchet." George's father instantly forgave him, telling him, "My son, that you should not be afraid to tell the truth is more to me than a thousand trees!"[1] George Washington was a real person, but the story of the cherry tree is a myth.

People still enjoy mythological monsters, too. You may have heard of Bigfoot, the Loch Ness Monster, alligators living in the sewers of New York City, or El Chupacabra, a doglike creature that sucks the blood out of unlucky livestock. Creatures like that let people feel that there are still secret and unexplored things on our planet—and they leave room for modern-day heroes to uncover them.

The Mythmakers

Ancient myths were recorded long ago, allowing people in modern times to study them. Homer's epic poems *The Iliad* and *The Odyssey* are among the oldest surviving written works by the Greeks. They've been dated anywhere from 1000 to 600 BCE, though most scholars agree they were written around 750 BCE. Scholars aren't sure if Homer was a real person. The name may have described a group of poets. However, for the sake of convenience, most refer to Homer as the author of both of these works.

Hesiod

The poems tell about the ten-year Trojan War and its aftermath. The attack on Troy by the Greeks might have happened, but we don't know that for certain. If it did, it probably took place in modern Turkey around 1100 BCE. Homer's tales tell of gods, kings, and heroes, and reveal daily life and beliefs of the Greeks and the Trojans.

Hesiod was another myth teller who lived around 700 BCE. He was a poor Greek farmer, but in his epic poem *Theogony* (thee-AHG-uh-nee), he ponders such lofty topics as gods and goddesses, humankind, and how the world began. *The Homeric Hymns* are thirty-three poems that honor various gods and goddesses. They were once attributed to Homer, but scholars now date the oldest of them to the seventh century BCE, decades after Homer lived. One hymn in the book may have been added as late as the sixth century BCE.

Roman poet Ovid compiled many of the Greek and Roman myths in their entirety. By 8 BCE, he had written *Metamorphoses,* which took up fifteen volumes. It catalogued Greek and Roman mythology from the beginning of the universe to the days of Julius Caesar, who was the leader of Rome until his assassination in 44 BCE.

Another collection of Greek myths is called *The Library,* or *Bibliotheca.* The author was once thought to be Apollodorus of Alexandria, a Greek scholar who lived around the second century BCE. Historians now say he didn't write it, so they attribute the *Bibliotheca* to pseudo-Apollodorus—or "resembling Apollodorus." The collection is long and detailed. Some readers say it's also extremely boring, unlike the lively accounts written by Ovid.

In 1821, Viennese professor and artist Johann Nepomuk Schaller sculpted Bellerophon slaying the Chimaera out of a large chunk of marble. The statue is nearly seven feet tall.

CHIMAERA

CHAPTER 3

A Monstrous Challenge

Bellerophon's heart was heavy. He had killed his brother in a hunting accident. Now he was exiled in Tiryns (ty-RINS) as a suppliant to the king.

The king's wife, Stheneboea (sthee-nee-BOY-uh), who is sometimes identified as Anteia (an-TY-uh), kept sliding up behind him and whispering about how she could help him forget his sorrow. Bellerophon (bel-AYR-uh-fon) wasn't interested. He had no intention of falling in love with a woman who was married to a powerful king.

"Please stop flirting with me," he finally told her. "Nothing is going to happen between us!"

The queen's feelings were hurt. Soon her sorrow turned to fury. She knew how to get even with the handsome and aloof Bellerophon. She raced to her king, but right before she entered his chamber, she pinched her cheeks so hard that tears came to her eyes. Then she walked in, her head bowed and her face flushed.

"What is it, my sweet?" King Proetus (proh-EE-tus) cried, when he saw how distressed she looked.

"Oh, my husband," she said, forcing out a sob. "It's that horrible Bellerophon! He tried to take advantage of me. I kept telling him to leave me alone, but he wouldn't. I had to fight him off!"

The king's blood boiled. He wanted to wring Bellerophon's neck, but he knew he couldn't. It simply wouldn't be polite to murder a houseguest.

Instead, the king came up with a plan.

"Do me a favor," he told the young warrior. "Deliver this sealed letter to King Iobates [eye-oh-BAY-teez], my wife's father in Lycia."

"Gladly! It's the least I can do to thank you for your hospitality," Bellerophon said, grinning happily. Secretly, he thought King Proetus was doing him a favor. It would be a relief to get away from Stheneboea, who was always mooning around, staring at him and sighing loudly.

When Bellerophon arrived in Lycia, King Iobates threw a nine-day party in his honor. On the tenth day, he asked for the letter Bellerophon had brought. The king read the letter with dismay. It said Bellerophon had tried to violate his daughter, and it asked Iobates to kill him.

Unfortunately, Iobates now had the same problem his son-in-law had experienced. He'd been entertaining Bellerophon for nearly two weeks. He couldn't kill a guest. It would anger the gods.

"Think, think, think!" he told himself, stuffing the letter into his tunic. He tried not to catch Bellerophon's eye as his brain raced. Then a brilliant idea came to him.

A monster called the Chimaera had been terrorizing Lycia and the surrounding countryside, eating people and livestock and turning everything in her path into smoldering ash. He would ask Bellerophon to kill the Chimaera. The young warrior didn't stand a chance against the fire-breathing, three-headed beast. He would die trying to take it down.

"Hey, Bellerophon," Iobates said casually. "I don't suppose you'd do me a big favor?"

Where Does the Chimaera Rear Her Three Heads?

Monsters and gods with animal parts had been around for some time when the Chimaera appeared in the work of two ancient Greek poets, Homer and Hesiod. In his epic poem *The Iliad,* Homer tells of Bellerophon's arrival in Lycia, and then describes the beast:

> So off he went to Lycia, safe in the escort of the gods, and once he reached the broad highlands cut by the rushing Xanthos, the king of Lycia gave him a royal welcome. Nine days he feasted him, nine oxen slaughtered. When the tenth Dawn shone with her rose-red fingers, he began to question him, asked to see his credentials, whatever he brought him from his in-law, Proetus. But then, once he received that fatal message sent from his own daughter's husband, first he ordered Bellerophon to kill the Chimaera—grim monster sprung of the gods, nothing human, all lion in front, all snake behind, all goat between, terrible, blasting lethal fire at every breath!"[1]

Hesiod's description didn't vary much from Homer's in his own epic poem, *Theogony*. Hesiod calls her the "Chimaera who breathed raging fire, a creature fearful, great, swift-footed and strong, who had three heads, one of a grim-eyed lion; in her hinderpart, a dragon; and in her middle, a goat, breathing forth a fearful blast of blazing fire."[2]

The Homeric Hymns briefly reference the Chimaera. After Apollo shoots a dragoness and she lies dying, he tells her: "Now rot here upon the soil that feeds man! You at least shall live no more to be a fell bane to men. . . . Against cruel death neither Typhoeus shall avail you nor ill-famed Chimera, but here shall the Earth and shining Hyperion [the sun] make you rot."[3]

Apollo slays the dragon Python. In *The Homeric Hymns*, she is equated with Echidna, the Chimaera's mother. However, by most human standards, Python is not quite as pretty as Echidna from the waist up.

By the fourth century BCE, people were beginning to dismiss the Chimaera myth as exactly that: a myth. In *Phaedrus,* Plato presents a dialogue between Socrates and Phaedrus. Socrates, a philosopher, has this to say about people who spend their time writing myths:

> Now I quite acknowledge that these allegories are very nice, but he is not to be envied who has to invent them; much labour and ingenuity will be required of him; and when he has once begun, he must go on and rehabilitate Hippocentaurs and chimeras dire. Gorgons and winged steeds flow in apace, and numberless other inconceivable and portentous natures.[4]

Around 50 BCE, Roman poet and philosopher Lucretius (loo-KREE-shus) warned people about believing in creatures like the Chimaera in his scientific poem *On the Nature of Things.* He writes that some things just can't be conjoined, or brought together in a single beast. When all things

In this English line drawing, the artist has given the Chimaera a goat's body, but no goat's head, and a snaky tail without a snake's head. Rendering something familiar in a new and different way is sometimes called artistic liberty.

This Chimaera has the typical heads—a lion's, goat's, and snake's—and a dragon's head to boot! It also has leathery batlike wings with talons. Artistic liberty could be a partial explanation for how mythical creatures change over centuries.

can be conjoined, he says, the world will be doomed. Therefore, he writes:

> Hulks of mankind half brute astarting up,
> At times big branches sprouting from man's trunk,
> Limbs of a sea-beast to a land-beast knit,
> And nature along the all-producing earth
> Feeding those dire Chimaeras breathing flame
> From hideous jaws—Of which 'tis simple fact
> That none have been begot.[5]

In the *Bibliotheca,* pseudo-Apollodorus provides a full account of the myth, with this description of the Chimaera: ". . . it was more than a match for many, let alone one; it had the fore part of a lion, the tail of a dragon, and its third head, the middle one, was that of a goat, through which it

In his epic poem *Aeneid,* written in the first century BCE, Roman poet Virgil describes the funeral games Aeneas throws for his father, Anchises, just after the Trojan War. The first event is a ship race. Virgil names the four ships in the race after fearsome creatures: *Scylla, Centaur, Pristis* (Shark), and *Chimera.*

belched fire. And it devastated the country and harried the cattle; for it was a single creature with the power of three beasts."6

Whether the ancient Greeks truly believed in the Chimaera, even at the time the stories about her were first told, we'll never know for sure. Perhaps some people did and others did not—just as today, some people search for the Loch Ness Monster or Bigfoot, while others simply grin at the thought of doing so.

Lycia—Land of Fire and Fury

The Lycians, who lived in what is today southern Turkey, were an ancient people with advanced ideas. They formed the Lycian League, one of the earliest democratic unions in history. Lycia's city-states may have been separated by steep mountains and deep gorges, but membership in the league united them in spirit.

The elected heads of each city-state had a vote in how the entire nation was run—something unheard of in the rest of the ancient world. This model was referred to in *The Federalist,* essays written in 1787 and 1788 by Alexander Hamilton, John Jay, and James Madison when they were trying to persuade New Yorkers to ratify the proposed United States Constitution.

While Greek city-states were often at war with each other, the Lycians enjoyed peace and prosperity. The Lycians had their own language before adopting Greek around the third century BCE. The Greeks and the Lycians traded goods—as well as stories and ideas. Lycia was the last region in the Mediterranean to be swallowed up by the Roman Empire, but even then its league continued to function.

The fires on Mount Yanartas in southern Turkey burn constantly. Even if they are smothered, they reignite. Some say these fires were the inspiration for the Chimaera myth.

Excavation on the parliament building in Patara where the league once met began in earnest around 1990. Hundreds of truckloads of sand have been carried from the ruins of the building, where Lycia's elected representatives sat so long ago in stone seats arranged in a semicircle.

Today tourists enjoy the beauty of the country by walking the Lycian Way, a 300-mile (500-km) footpath marked with red-and-white stripes every hundred yards or so. The stunningly beautiful hike winds through thick forests, over hills, across ancient ruins, and into the Hidden City Gorge, the deepest gorge in Turkey. Views of the sparkling Mediterranean Sea can be seen from many parts of the trail.

A 20-foot mural painted by Venetian artist Giovanni Battista Tiepolo on a ceiling in the Palazzo Labia in Venice, Italy, shows Bellerophon atop the winged horse Pegasus.

CHIMAERA

CHAPTER 4

Dreaming of Death

Bellerophon approached the pillared temple of the goddess Athena (ah-THEE-nah). The words of Polyeidus (pah-lee-EYE-dus) still echoed in his mind. The seer had given him the secret to fighting the Chimaera. Bellerophon needed to capture the flying horse Pegasus and ride him above her, then rain his weapons down on the beast.

Bellerophon had doubts about how he would carry out the plan. He had long admired Pegasus, a beautiful white horse with huge wings. But no man could stay on the wild steed's back.

Polyeidus told him that to capture and ride Pegasus, he needed to ask Athena, the goddess of wisdom, for help. Bellerophon entered the stone temple, his footsteps echoing in the huge, empty space. He knelt before the altar.

"Please, goddess, I need you," he whispered. "Help me capture Pegasus so that I can slay the Chimaera." He stretched out on the cool stone floor, still praying quietly. Soon he fell into a deep sleep.

"Bellerophon!" he heard a sweet voice call. A figure emerged from the darkness and stood before him. A soft light glowed around the beautiful woman. "You'll need this to catch Pegasus," Athena said. She pulled something from her peplos—it was a golden bridle. Bellerophon wondered how she'd kept the bulky bridle hidden under her sheer, form-fitting garment.

He lurched awake. It had only been a dream, he realized, as early morning light seeped into the temple. He sat up and his hand brushed against something. He looked down. There, next to him on the floor, was a golden bridle. The dream had been real. Athena had delivered what he needed to catch and ride the winged horse.

"Yes!" he cried triumphantly. "Victory will be mine."

Bellerophon couldn't wait to be a hero.

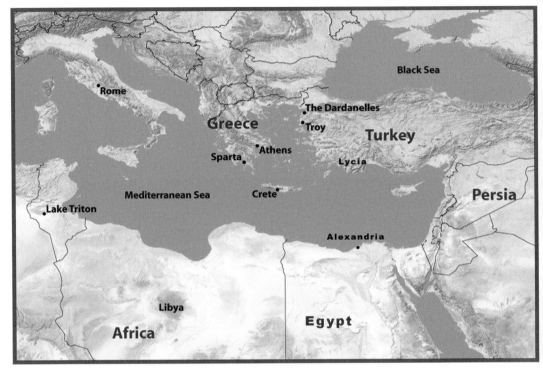

The Mediterranean Sea laps at the shores of Italy, Greece, Turkey, the Middle East, Africa, and other places.

The Meaning of the Myth

To understand the birth of the Chimaera myth, let your imagination roam back thousands of years. Imagine looking down on the islands of Greece lying cradled in the blue waters of the Mediterranean Sea. To the north lies Lycia, a region in today's southern Turkey. To the south lies the continent of Africa, with the city of Alexandria at the tip of Egypt. To the east lies the huge region of Mesopotamia—the land between the Tigris and Euphrates rivers. On the banks of these rivers are Sumeria, birthplace of writing and the wheel and known as the Cradle of Civilization, and Babylon, with its famous hanging gardens. (Today, Mesopotamia is Iraq, northeastern parts of Syria, and some parts of Turkey and Iran.)

Ancient people traveled throughout these regions to trade goods for things they couldn't produce themselves. They warred with each other to gain power and land. For example, in 331 BCE, Macedonian ruler Alexander the Great conquered Babylon. While the people fought and traded, they also exchanged ideas and stories.

Over time, there have been many versions of the Chimaera myth, with just as many meanings. Different people interpret it different ways. Even the Chimaera herself changes. Sometimes her snake tail is a dragon instead. Sometimes she has wings.

Some stories say the Chimaera represented a mountain in Lycia, located in today's southern Turkey and within easy sailing distance from Greece. The ancient Mount Chimaera may have been one that is known today as Yanartas. It has several vents that emit burning methane, much the way the Chimaera's mouth emitted flames. In ancient times, the vents were landmarks sailors used to navigate safely. Mount Chimaera was said to have snakes at its base, goat pastures in the middle, and savage lions roaming at the top, near its eternally burning fire.

Robert Graves suggested in his book *Greek Myths* that the three heads of the Chimaera represented the three seasons of the year—spring, summer, and winter—as it was divided in ancient times. He writes: "A Chimaera has been found carved on the walls of a Hittite temple at Carchemish and, like such other composite beasts as the Sphinx and the Unicorn, will originally have been a calendar symbol: each component represented a season of the Queen of Heaven's sacred year—as, according to Diodorus Siculus, the three strings of her tortoise-shell lyre also did."[1]

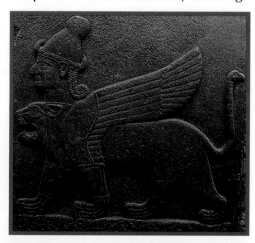

Carchemish was a city on the border of today's Turkey and Syria, and it was the location of an epic battle between the Babylonians and the Egyptians. It is mentioned several times in the Bible.

Graves suggests that the myth represented the shift from a time when religion embraced the

A carving on a temple wall at Carchemish shows a winged lion with a head rising from its back and a tail with a bird of prey at its tip.

feminine and became more patriarchal—or led by men: "Bellerophon masters winged Pegasus and kills the Chimaera. Perseus, in a variant on the same legend, flies through the air and beheads Pegasus's mother, the Gorgon Medusa; much as Marduk, a Babylonian hero, kills the she-monster Tiamet, goddess of the Sea. Perseus . . . represented the patriarchal Hellenes who invaded Greece and Asia Minor early in the second millennium BC, and challenged the power of the Triple-goddess. . . . [Bellerophon] Perseus's double, kills the Lycian Chimaera: that is, the Hellenes annulled the ancient Medusan calendar and replaced it with another,"[2] Graves writes.

An Italian professor named Ugo Bardi is an expert on the mythical creature. He agrees with Graves about the Chimaera myth springing from a time when power shifted from goddesses to gods. "What is the myth really about? Ancient authors of classical times asked themselves this question, too,"[3] writes Bardi, and he guesses at the answer by going back in time.

He refers to a 1934 paper called "The Representation of the Chimaera," in which the author, Anne Roes, says the position and the shape of the goat's head may be a misrepresentation of what was originally a pair of wings.[4]

"So, the origin of the myth may have been a winged lion," Bardi speculates. "Lions lived as far north as Greece and Italy in very ancient times,

Winged lion in Venice

but really they were best known in North Africa and in Mesopotamia. We have beautiful images of kings hunting and killing lions all over Egypt and Babylon. And we do have images of winged lions."[5]

Some of those images date back to the end of the third millennium BCE. But to explore the birth of the myth, we have to go back even farther, to the Sumerian civilization, which started as early as the fifth millennium BCE.

Bardi examines a clay Sumerian cylinder seal from around 3500 BCE. It shows a winged lion pulling a cart, in which a godlike figure rides. Standing on top of the lion is a goddess holding what looks like lightning bolts. At the lion's head, a welcoming figure offers a drink. The lion spews something from its mouth, possibly the rain or lightning that comes with a storm.

"There is no monster here, and no armor-clad Bellerophon . . . ," Bardi says. "This lion is a thunder beast, the embodiment of a storm.

Clay Sumerian cylinder seal, about 5,500 years old

The whole image seems to symbolize the fertilization of the land, with the sun chariot coming after the storm beast."[6]

The demise of the Sumerian and Babylonian cultures saw the myth morph into something entirely different. "The female Goddess became a male God, the benign creature an evil one," Bardi says. On the Sumerian cylinder, the lines "that go out of the mouth of the beast as fertilizing water, in later times became arrows or bolts going into the mouth of the creature as killing weapons."[7]

The rebirth of the myth, he continues, represents the change from "a goddess-ruled system to a male dominated system. . . . The winged lion, the storm beast of Sumerian times, ceased to be a symbol of fertilization and became an evil monster. The goddess, she who rode the lion and [who sometimes was] a lioness, became, too, an evil creature."[8]

The goat head on the Chimaera

Turning the lion's wings into a goat's head was not by chance, Bardi adds. Chimaera, which means "she-goat," might be based on a verbal confusion. The word "storm" is *cheimon* in ancient Greek. He also points to the symbology of the goat itself: "Goats, male or female, are not common as monsters, but in the Christian myth of the devil, as well as in the Greek one of the Satyrs, the goat element seems to be meant to evidence the 'unclean' nature of the creature. This uncleanliness seems to be the main reason of the appearance on the Chimaera's back of the goat together with the snake, another malignant creature in most mythologies. . . . The Chimaera is in the end a grotesque and deformed image of the mother goddess and it embodies all the evil that men can think about women."[9]

The creature that has so thoroughly captured Bardi's imagination is "no mere monster," he tells us. "It is a reflection of unbelievably ancient stories, stories that involve some of the most powerful symbols and concepts that act on the human mind: the snake, the dragon, the mother, fertility, the thunder, the hero's quest, the slaying of the evil one."[10]

The details of life are ever-changing and that means our stories are ever-changing, too. Wars begin and end. Power switches from one leader's hands to another's. Goddesses are in favor, and then gods are in favor, and then there is only one god, and then, for some people, there are no gods at all. One day art is made showing a winged lion that brings rain for crops. Centuries later, another lion is a man-eating she-monster with three heads.

Some things haven't changed in the last several thousand years, however. People still like to talk about what they believe in. And they love to tell stories and hear them told.

Pegasus

Pegasus, the immortal flying horse with a shining white coat and wings, was born from one of the most frightening monsters in Greek mythology. His mother, Medusa, was one of the three Gorgons (which comes from the Greek word *gorgós,* meaning "dreadful"). The Gorgons were sisters with hair of snakes and gazes that turned to stone anyone who dared to look into their eyes.

Two of the sisters were immortal, but Medusa was not, and a hero named Perseus entered her cave to kill her. He used the polished shield of the goddess Athena to view Medusa's reflection so that she couldn't turn him to stone. Then he cut off her head with Athena's sword. Medusa's blood spilled into the ocean, which was ruled by the god Poseidon. It mixed with white sea foam, and Pegasus was born.

Pegasus was a frisky horse who did not like to be ridden, but he was tamed by Bellerophon. The hero slipped a golden bridle over the steed's head to gain control of him. Then Bellerophon climbed onto the winged horse's back, and the two rose into the sky and flew until they found the Chimaera.

Pegasus bore Bellerophon on two other deadly quests set by King Iobates—against the warlike Solymi and the Amazons. According to some myths, Bellerophon also used Pegasus to drop Stheneboea into the sea as punishment for starting all his troubles. After these successes, he decided to pay the gods on Mount Olympus a visit. He felt he was their equal. Zeus saw Bellerophon and Pegasus flying higher and higher toward his heavenly abode. Angered by

Pegasus

Bellerophon's arrogance, he sent a gadfly to bite Pegasus, who bucked when he was stung. Bellerophon fell off and crashed to the earth. He was hurt so badly that he spent the rest of his days crippled, blind, and friendless.

Zeus took Pegasus for himself, and used the horse to carry his thunderbolts. He set him in the sky as a constellation.

An attack from above heralds the fate of the Chimaera.

CHIMAERA

CHAPTER 5

The Chimaera's Fire Dies

The Chimaera walked out of her cave into the sunlight. She took a deep breath of fresh air. Then she bounded down the mountainside, dodging trees and rocks, and enjoying the feel of the sun on her back.

"Wheeeeee!" bleated her goat's head, its beard flying in the wind.

The Chimaera would have to run long and hard to reach the distant village she had in mind. She had scouted it from the edge of the woods but had never entered it, so she knew the people would not be expecting her. She planned to rush into its center and snatch every living creature she could find.

What she really craved was a lamb. She loved how tender lamb flesh tasted after she charred it a bit with her fiery breath. That was what she would eat first, she thought. A trickle of drool escaped her mouth and blew away on the wind.

When she arrived on the outskirts of the village, she paused for a moment. Then she launched herself with her scaly hindquarters and began her attack. As she lunged, she felt a sharp arrow bounce off her shoulder. She glanced around in annoyance.

A white horse was flying above her, with a puny human astride it. She snarled angrily and kept running. More arrows rained down on her, but they couldn't pierce her rock-hard hide. She entered the village, glancing around for a sheep pen. Her stomach rumbled with hunger, and pebbles skittered under her feet as she slid to a stop.

Just then, the horse swooped low over her head. The Chimaera crouched and looked up, growling angrily. The human on the horse was holding something—it looked like a long spear with a blob on the end.

She snarled in rage and let out a blast of fire. Just then, the human thrust the spear into her mouth. The Chimaera's yellow eyes opened wide in surprise. The spear had a ball of iron on its tip. Her hot breath melted it into scalding liquid. She could feel the molten metal eating through her throat and stomach.

She tried to rear up and swat the horse and its grinning rider out of the sky, but her body was becoming weak. She wobbled, trying to keep her balance. Her legs gave out and she collapsed to the ground.

She lifted her head and tried to growl, but her throat was closed up. No fire would spew from her mouth. Tears welled in her eyes as she curled into a ball, hoping the terrible pain would stop. A final thought entered her mind: How good a charred lamb would have tasted on this fine day! Her snake tail twitched, then lay still. Her goat's head sighed and rested on her back. The Chimaera closed her yellow eyes for the last time.

This German mural of Bellerophon thrusting a spear into the Chimaera's throat is by August Ferdinand Hopfengarten, who lived in the 1800s.

The Chimaera of Arezzo

The Chimaera of Arezzo is a dramatic statue that was made about 2,400 years ago. It stands two and a half feet high, and it crouches and snarls at an unseen attacker. It is one of the few remaining large bronze statues made by the Etruscans, an ancient people who had their own language. They had lived in Etruria—in today's central Italy—since prehistoric times.

Workers found the statue over 450 years ago, in 1553, when they were digging trenches next to the walls of the city of Arezzo. It had been buried there long before that, for safekeeping, along with several smaller bronze statues. The Etruscans might have been trying to protect it from invading Romans who took over Etruria in the centuries before Jesus was born.

The city's archives have notes from the time of the discovery about how impressed the townspeople were by the fine statue of a "lion," which was missing its tail. Pieces of the tail—in the shape of a snake—were discovered a short time later, but a new tail wasn't crafted and attached until the eighteenth century. The tail let people know for sure that the statue was of a Chimaera. As the Getty Museum notes, "Its defensive posture suggests that it was originally part of a larger sculptural group that included Bellerophon and Pegasus."[1]

The Grand Duke of Tuscany was a patron of the arts, and the minute he heard about the discovery, he ordered the statue be moved to the Palazzo Vecchio in Florence. There, the public could marvel at it. (The handsome duke also took advantage of his powerful position to have all the smaller statues moved to his home, the Palazzo Pitti, where he enjoyed cleaning off the dirt and rust and examining the pieces closely.)

We still have questions about who made the statue. At the time it was created, the Etruscans were trading with the Greeks, whose culture and artistic style had a profound influence on them. The Chimaera might have been sculpted by a Greek craftsman living in Etruria. It has telltale signs of the Greek style, including the realistic way the lion's body is formed. However, the raised muscles over its bulging eyes are a hallmark of Etruscan artists. The orderly, stylized mane is also at odds with the natural-looking lion's body.

The Chimaera of Arezzo is a prime example of Etruscan bronze statuary and one of very few large pieces to have survived from that time. It is displayed at the National Archaeological Museum in Florence, Italy.

The statue has an inscription on its right foreleg that gives us a good idea of its original purpose. It has been read different ways, but most people today agree that it says TINSCVIL. That means it was likely a votive object to be set in a sacred place, like a temple, in order to please the supreme Etruscan god Tin, or Tinia.

The Chimaera was moved from the Palazzo Vecchio in the eighteenth century and placed in the nearby Uffizi Gallery, where it got its new tail. In the nineteenth century, the Chimaera was moved again to its current home, the National Archaeological Museum in Florence, Italy, where it is one of the first things visitors see. Replicas of the statue are located in various places, including one at the spot where the original was found, and two in front of the Arezzo train station.

In an article about the Chimaera of Arezzo, Ugo Bardi points out that the statue is different from the many painted and sculpted Chimaeras made during classical times. "In most of these images, the Chimaera may be lively and full of movement, or it may be rigid and stiff, but never [does it have] the expressive intensity of the Arezzo one. . . . The fiery, fire-breathing monster is shown as a lean, perhaps hungry, creature in a moment of suffering. The body is curled in a posture that reminds [us] of an angry cat, while the mouth is open as if screaming, [and] the goat's head is reclining down and drops of blood appear on the neck."[2]

Bardi says it may be hard for modern people to understand why a religious offering would be a three-headed monster. It highlights the way people's thinking has changed in the 2,500 years since the statue was made and admired. However, the ideas that drove the artist to make the statue may not be so different from the urges that drive today's people to express themselves.

It's interesting to wonder how an ancient story was born, and many great thinkers—like Bardi, Graves, Hamilton and others—have spent long, happy hours doing so. It's also interesting to wonder how today's stories will be perceived by people living thousands of years in the future. For instance, will they read all the books that have recently been written about zombies and wonder if people of the twenty-first century were afraid of a zombie uprising? Perhaps a child of the future will curl up with a book and guess about what we believe in today. As with any story or myth, much will likely be left to the imagination.

The Chimaera Today

Today the word *chimera* can mean something you hope for but will never get. It also refers to a wild or unrealistic dream or idea.

Scientists use the word to describe an animal or plant that has genes from two different species. Researchers have created the OncoMouse, which contains a human cancer gene. It was patented in 1988 by Harvard scientists and is used for cancer research. The word also describes a virus containing genetic material from other organisms.

There is an ancient deep-sea fish related to sharks that is called the chimaera.

Chimera is the name of a World Wide Web browser. It's also the name of a graphics program that lets people build images of tiny molecules. The name is used for companies, like one that makes lights used for films and videos.

Chimaera fish

The Chimaera rears her heads in many pop-culture places. She appears in video games, on television shows, and in movies. She shows up in role-playing games, like Dungeons

The Chimaera

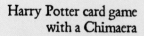

Power Rangers version of the Chimaera

and Dragons. She appears on television series, like *Mighty Morphin' Power Rangers, CSI: Crime Scene Investigation, Star Trek,* and *X-Files,* and she is referred to in books, including the Harry Potter series.

The Chimaera has also had guest spots in many video games, including the Final Fantasy series, Resident Evil 4, Resistance: Fall of Man, and World of Warcraft.

It's even the name of an Irish band and a heavy metal band from Cleveland called Chimaira. The name is also used for many albums and songs.

Just as many of the names and stories from ancient Greek myths live on, the Chimaera is still with us today, making us realize that many things in life are made up of more than one simple part.

Harry Potter card game with a Chimaera

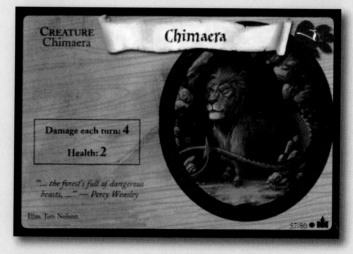

CREATURE
Chimaera

Chimaera

Damage each turn: 4

Health: 2

"... the forest's full of dangerous beasts, ..." — Percy Weasley

Illus. Jim Nelson

57/80

Chapter 1. A Beautiful Baby

1. Apollodorus, *The Library*, translated by Sir James George Frazer (New York: G. P. Putnam's Sons, 1921), Book 1, p. 47.

2. Holy Bible, Job 41: 14–34, King James Version.

3. Michael Delahoyde and Katherine S. McCartney, *"Monsters in Classical Mythology,"* Washington State University, http://www.wsu.edu/~delahoyd/monsters.html

4. Ibid.

5. Ibid.

6. Ibid.

7. Edith Hamilton, *Mythology*, Boston, New York, London: Little, Brown and Company, 1942; First Back Bay Paperback Edition, 1998, p. 12.

8. Ibid., p. 9

9. Ibid., pp. 9–10

10. Ibid., p. 10

11. Ibid., p. 12

Chapter 2. A Time to Feast

1. M. L. Weems, *The Cherry Tree*, Apples4theteacher.com, http://www.apples4theteacher.com/holidays/presidents-day/george-washington/short-stories/the-cherry-tree.html

Chapter 3. A Monstrous Challenge

1. Homer, *The Iliad*, translated by Robert Fagles (New York: Penguin Classics, 1990), Book 6, lines 203-216.

2. Hesiod, *Theogony*, translated by Hugh G. Evelyn-White, lines 306—332, http://www.sacred-texts.com/cla/hesiod/theogony.htm

3. *Homeric Hymn to Pythian Apollo*, translated by Hugh G. Evelyn-White (New York: G.P. Putnam's Sons, 1914), lines 361–387.

4. Plato, *Phaedrus*, translated by Benjamin Jowett, http://classics.mit.edu/Plato/phaedrus.html

5. Lucretius, *On the Nature of Things*, translated by William Ellery Leonard, Book II, http://classics.mit.edu/Carus/nature_things.2.ii.html

6. Apollodorus, *The Library*, translated by Sir James George Frazer, (New York: G. P. Putnam's Sons, 1921), Book II, pp. 149–153.

Chapter 4. Dreaming of Death

1. Robert Graves, *The Greek Myths*, http://www.scribd.com/doc/13794098/Robert-Graves-The-Greek-Myths

2. Ibid.

3. Ugo Bardi, Chimaera: *A Site Dedicated to the Chimaera (or Chimera) Myth*, "Chimaera: The Origins of the Myth," http://www1.unifi.it/surfchem/solid/bardi/chimera/origins.html

4. Ibid.

5. Ibid.

6. Ibid.

7. Ibid.

8. Ibid.

9. Ibid.

10. Ibid.

Chapter 5. The Chimaera's Fire Dies

1. The Getty Museum, *"The Chimaera of Arezzo*, (Getty Villa Exhibitions)," http://www.getty.edu/art/exhibitions/chimaera/english.html

2. Ugo Bardi, *Chimaera: A Site Dedicated to the Chimaera (or Chimera) Myth*, "The Chimaera of Arezzo," http://www1.unifi.it/surfchem/solid/bardi/chimera/chimarezzo.html

Books

Church, Alfred J. *The Iliad for Boys and Girls*. Chapel Hill, N.C.: Yesterday's Classics, 2006.

Cobblestone Publishing. *If I Were a Kid in Ancient Greece* . . . Peterborough, N.H.: Cricket Books, 2007.

Golding, Julia. *The Chimera's Curse*. Tarrytown, N.Y.: Marshall Cavendish, 2008.

Macfarlane, Stuart and Linda. *Medusa Island*. Glendale, Calif.: DNA Press and Nartea Publishing, 2008.

Works Consulted

Apollodorus (Pseudo). *The Library*. Translated by Sir James George Frazer. New York: G. P. Putnam's Sons, 1921.

Bardi, Ugo. *Chimaera: A Site Dedicated to the Chimaera (or Chimera) Myth*. April 2007. http://www1.unifi.it/surfchem/solid/bardi/chimera/index.html

Bernstein, Richard. "A Congress, Buried in Turkey's Sand." *The New York Times,* September 19, 2005. http://www.nytimes.com/2005/09/19/international/europe/19patara.html?_r=1&8hpib&oref=login

Delahoyde, Michael, and Katherine S. McCartney. "Monsters in Classical Mythology." Washington State University. http://www.wsu.edu/~delahoyd/monsters.html

The Getty Museum. "The Chimaera of Arezzo (Getty Villa Exhibitions)." http://www.getty.edu/art/exhibitions/chimaera/english.html

Graves, Robert. *Greek Myths*. London: Penguin Books, 1981; also online at http://www.scribd.com/doc/13794098/Robert-Graves-The-Greek-Myths

Hamilton, Edith. *Mythology*. Boston, New York, London: Little, Brown and Company, 1942; First Back Bay Paperback Edition, 1998.

Hesiod. *Theogony*. Translated by Hugh G. Evelyn-White, 1914. http://www.sacred-texts.com/cla/hesiod/theogony.htm

Holy Bible. King James Version.

Homeric Hymn to Pythian Apollo. Translated by Hugh G. Evelyn-White. New York: G.P. Putnam's Sons, 1914. http://www.theoi.com/Text/HomericHymns1.html

Homer. *The Iliad*. Translated by Robert Fagles. New York: Penguin Classics, 1990.

Isaac, James, and Jane Smith. "What Is a Myth?" 1999; revised July 2006 by Joan Jahnige. http://www.dl.ket.org/latin1/mythology/whatisa.htm

CHIMAERA

"The Labors of Hercules." Perseus Digital Library, Tufts University; Gregory R. Crane, Editor-in-Chief. http://www.perseus.tufts.edu/Herakles/labors.html

LeDoux, Joseph. *The Emotional Brain*. New York: Simon & Schuster Paperbacks, 1996.

Lucretius. *On the Nature of Things*. Translated by William Ellery Leonard (1916). http://classics.mit.edu/Carus/nature_things.2.ii.html

McPhee, Isaac M. "The Chimera, Then and Now." February 2008. http://greek-history.suite101.com/article.cfm/the_chimera_then_and_now

Plato. *Phaedrus*. Translated by Benjamin Jowett. http://classics.mit.edu/Plato/phaedrus.html

Pliny the Elder. *The Natural History*. Ed. John Bostock. http://www.perseus.tufts.edu/hopper/text?doc=Perseus:text:1999.02.0137:book=13:chapter=21

Safyurek, Patty, and Kemal Safyurek. "Lycian Turkey—Discover the Beauty of Ancient Lycia." http://www.lycianturkey.com/index.htm

Theoi Greek Mythology. The Theoi Project. http://www.theoi.com

Weems, M. L. *The Cherry Tree*. http://www.apples4theteacher.com/holidays/presidents-day/george-washington/short-stories/the-cherry-tree.html

On the Internet

Mythical Creatures & Beasts
http://www.mythicalcreaturesguide.com

Mythological Monsters
http://monsters.monstrous.com/index.htm

afterlife—A state of being after death.

allegory (AL-uh-gor-ee)—A story, poem, or picture with a hidden meaning.

ancient (AYN-shunt)—Belonging to the distant past.

appendage (uh-PEN-dudj)—Something attached to something larger; arms and legs are appendages to the body.

archaeologist (ar-kee-AH-luh-jist)—A person who studies what other people did in the past.

bestial (BES-chul)—Like an animal.

classical period—In history, a broad term for a long period of time centered on the Mediterranean Sea and the civilizations of ancient Greece and Rome.

composite (kom-PAH-zit)—Made up of different parts.

exiled (EK-zyld)—Barred from one's native country.

Hellenes (HEL-enz)—The ancient Greeks.

Hittite (HIH-tyt)—A member of an ancient people who established an empire in Asia Minor and Syria that flourished from around 1700 to 1200 BCE.

incomprehensibilities (in-kom-pree-hen-sih-BIL-ih-teez)—Things that are impossible to understand.

lyre—A stringed instrument like a small U-shaped harp.

Mediterranean (meh-dih-ter-AY-nee-un)—The Mediterranean Sea and the countries surrounding it, including Egypt, Turkey, Syria, and Greece.

meed—A deserved share.

millennium (mil-EH-nee-um)—A period of a thousand years.

nymph (NIMF)—A mythological spirit of nature.

omnipotent (om-NIH-puh-tunt)—All powerful.

peplos (PEP-lohs)—An outer robe worn by women in ancient Greece.

rational (RAA-shuh-nul)—Logical; clear thinking.

seer (SEE-ur)—Someone who can see the future.

stylized (STY-lyzd)—Depicted in an unrealistic way.

suppliant (SUH-plee-unt)—A person who makes a humble plea to someone with authority.

CHIMAERA

PHOTO CREDITS: Cover, p. 1—Joe Rasemas; p. 9—Gustav Doré; pp. 10, 14, 18, 24–26, 30–34, 36—Creative Commons 2.0; p. 12—Barbara Marvis; p. 17—Michelangelo Caravaggio; p. 20—Johann Wilhelm Baur; p. 28—Giovanni Battista Tiepolo. Every effort has been made to locate all copyright holders of material used in this book. If any errors or omissions have occurred, corrections will be made in future editions of this book.